PUBLISHED by PARABLES
Earthly Stories with a Heavenly Meaning

This Book Is Dedicated to The Wonderful Three That Have Blessed My Life the Most: Heavenly Father, Lord Jesus Christ and Holy Spirit and to the people who read this book.

God bless you all.

GIFTS TO THE GIVER
~The Early Years~

By
Monika Starr Langguth

GIFTS TO THE GIVER ~The Early Years ~
Monika Starr Langguth

Published By Parables
May, 2019

All Rights Reserved. No part of this book may be reproduced or utilized in any form or by any means, electronic or mechanical, including photocopying, recording, or by any information storage and retrieval system, without permission in writing from the author.

    ISBN 978-1-945698-57-6
    Printed in the United States of America

Readers should be aware that Internet Web sites offered as citations and/or sources for further information may have been changed or disappeared between the time this was written and the time it is read.

GIFTS TO THE GIVER
~The Early Years~

By
Monika Starr Langguth

Monika Starr Langguth

INTRODUCTION

Gifts to The Giver ~ The Early Years

This book has been a long time coming. Not because I wasn't anxious to see it come to fruition, but I needed to grow and mature and get myself out of the way. Even though we think we are ready and humble and "God gets the Glory," God helps us learn patience and perseverance and real humility. He keeps us in a kind of "suspension" while He puts us over and over again into the fire. It gets hot and sometimes we want to give up. Like the blacksmith that first allows the metal to be red hot, then he can shape it. Or the glassblower that melts the glass to form a magnificent piece of art, The Master Artist uses the fire of His Love and discipline to mold us into something we never thought we could be ... but He did!
Let's say we're swimming in the ocean ... we are halfway there, so what is our plan? Swim back, keep going or drown? Everyone must answer that for themselves.

I chose to keep swimming and finally I saw the shoreline and then the next part of the journey begins. Once I learned that we are traveling through and that our destination is Heaven, I understood rest areas are not my permanent residence. I made my decision to keep going forward and heeding the directions of Heaven's GPS: "God's Perfect Strategist," The Holy Spirit of God. His strategies are brilliant and yet many times along the road of life, we turn the volume down and start on roads with detours up ahead. But, if we turn up the volume, we hear, "Make a U-turn" and we get back on track. It's called repentance and we change direction. Hopefully after a while, we keep our spirits tuned into God's frequency so we can travel well.

Gifts To The Giver ~The Early Years~

All my life I have loved to write and create things with words. Commercials fascinated me and so I'd create my own while shampooing my hair or eating a sandwich. Funny little aside, many years later a few of the names of my products were used in the hair industry! Wait! Where are my royalties? Many a poem was written to friends about silly things that happened... like throwing up after a rollercoaster ride. I told you they were silly!
Before I truly knew Jesus as my Savior and Lord, my writings were very sad. That revelation came when I found and read them many years later. Back then I didn't realize how sad they were, but since writing exposes the soul, like it or not, it was truth revealed. I was a broken person and my writings uncovered what I thought I was doing such a good job of hiding. Then along came Jesus and my soul sang a new song; a young and immature song, but a song nevertheless. It was a love song I was singing to God, though in my heart, I believe I was echoing His heart to mine. And a new and amazing journey began.

I pray that you will be blessed by these writings. I must tell you honestly, they are not mine. Just like the parable of the talents in the 35th Chapter of Matthew, God gives us unrefined gifts. In truth, that really is a two-sided coin, because what God gives us is perfect, it's just in the hands of imperfect beings it takes time to figure out. For example, the difference between oil paints placed in the hands of a disciplined artist and that of a two-year old. What a wonderful and funny God we serve! I am reviewing this one more time before publication and He told me to put in the words, "two-sided coin" and the parable in Matthew is about talents and they were coins!!! See why I love Him so much? He's the Best Editor we can ever have!!

My prayer is that you will be encouraged to release the song in your own soul. Perhaps you already have. The song within each one of us brings something forth to cheer on another runner to finish the race and finish it strong. We are all in this together and unity brings great glory to Our Father

Monika Starr Langguth

in Heaven Who loves us beyond human comprehension. When we sing our songs as one, The Father leans forward to listen and the angels become silent. Angels are very important, but we are His Children. Just watch the face of a parent at a school play beaming with pride – "that's my kid singing!" We learned that from Our Father in Heaven.

I must warn you that I am not the most orthodox person on the planet. Over the years I have come to understand that is how I was created. After all, if God made creatures with big long trunks and striped horses and polka dotted long neck giraffes, can you imagine how diverse His children are? See! Now you must feel better because that includes you! You, yes you! You are one of a kind! God doesn't make copies. Why? Because He is a Creator and not a duplicator! For example, DNA, fingerprints and snowflakes . . . no two are alike. And, if you find two the same, let me know.

Why I wrote this book.
It wasn't until I was preparing to submit for publication, that God revealed to my heart why this book was so important to Him.
Since I have been writing for over 30 years, I began thinking that these older works were rather "yesterday's news," so I inquired of The Lord whether I should even put them in print. After all, I have come so far . . . and these?

It's amazing how "self" is constantly resisting "The Spirit" just like a kid who wants to get his hand out of Mommy's while crossing the street. "I'm a big boy/girl now!" God burdened my heart to remember that 'All things have beginnings." If He thought it was so important to reveal to us, "In the Beginning," then shouldn't I, too, begin at the beginning? Even after 30 years, God must straighten us out once in a while.

What you are presently holding is a compilation of the writings of a new believer just learning the ways of God; a fledgling in her faith, yet totally

Gifts To The Giver ~The Early Years ~

overwhelmed with the wonder and beauty and love of This newly discovered God.

While these writings may seem to lack the depth of a seasoned believer, they are filled with the joy and excitement of finding The One Who loves us beyond what we can ever experience from another living soul.

This is a book for all those that may have just found "The Lover of Their Souls" or for those that have known Him for a long time and can look back and remember the emotions they felt when they met their "Eternal True Love." Most remember meeting their first love in the earthly realm; and then that born-again experience when they met "Love Himself," Jesus Christ, the divine and human expression of The Invisible God.

So, I pray that you, dear reader, will be blessed and encouraged to draw from the wells of your own memories. Some of these poems and stories may make you laugh and sometimes cry. If they touch your heart, I hope you will share with those that are just starting out on their journey with the Father through Jesus Christ, His Son. Of course, we all have our own personal experience and relationship with God, but I truly believe our awareness and revelation of "Who He Is" expands when we hear how another one of His children sees and experiences this wondrous God.

This is the first of a series. As each book comes forth, hopefully the reader will observe growth and increased depth of insight into the things of God through His Holy Spirit penned by His humble scribe. This faithful third Person of the Godhead is our constant companion, revealing more and more of who we are and "Whose we are" as we time-travel on earth to our destination, Heaven, our Eternal Home.

God bless you and I thank you for taking time to see through another's eyes how God has revealed Himself as Our Wonderful Heavenly Father. The

Monika Starr Langguth

Ultimate Giver. The Giver of Life. The Giver of Jesus. The Giver of All Good Gifts. As I grew in my understanding of how wonderful "This Giver" is, I felt there was nothing I could give to Him of worth in comparison. But as I relentlessly pursued This Glorious Giver in prayer, He revealed to me that the only thing He truly wanted, He could not have unless I gave it to Him. That gift was my heart.

And Dear Child of God, that's all He wants from you . . . your love.

I am sending this book out with my love. You may ask, how can I love you if I don't even know you? It's simple! If I love God Whom I cannot see (in the natural) why can't I love those whom I do not see, but God loves? That's my story and I'm sticking to it!

So here we go! Thank you for coming with me on this journey. I look forward to hearing from you someday. If not here on planet Earth, when we get Home to Heaven for Our Eternal Family Reunion.

May this gift be pleasing to You, Dear Father, here is my heart.

And to you, dear reader, may God richly bless you in Jesus' Name and in His Love,

Monika

TGBTG ~ To God Be The Glory

Last word:
There are hundreds of translations for this scripture, but I felt led to use this simple precious one:

James 1:17- Easy-to-Read Version (ERV)
Everything good comes from God. Every perfect gift is from Him. These good gifts come down from the Father Who made all the lights in the sky. But God never changes like the shadows from those lights. He is always the

Gifts To The Giver ~The Early Years~

same. God decided to give us life through the true message He sent to us. He wanted us to be the most important of all that He created.

Monika Starr Langguth

GIFTS TO THE GIVER

Whatever Could I Give You, God
You Don't Already Own?
The Earth, The Very Universe:
A Footstool for Your Throne.

What Can I Give? Just Look at Me
A Fragile Piece of Clay
And Still, I Feel You're Wanting More
What Have I to Repay?

All I Have You Gave to Me
You Are My Only Source
Yet, there is More You're Longing For
But Will Not Take by Force.

"The Gifts I Gave... They Now Are Yours
To Do with As You Will"
Louder Pumped My Yearning Heart
As Silent Came My Still.

Gifts To The Giver ~The Early Years~

"Listen... And You'll Understand
I Want What You Can Be
But All the Gifts I Gave to You
Your Heart Must Give to Me.
You See, Your Heart Belongs to You

It Listens to Your Voice
Yet, If You Speak, 'Lord, All Is Yours'
Your Gift Will Be Your Choice."
So Now I've Come to Understand

What I Can Now Impart
This is The Gift You Want from Me
I Give to You, My Heart.

Monika Starr Langguth
TGBTG
2005©

Monika Starr Langguth

INDEX

OUR SON
A READY WRITER
BEAUTY ETERNAL
BE NOT SLEEPING
THANK YOU, FATHER, FOR MY MOTHER
ONE DAY IN HEAVEN
DADDY'S LITTLE GIRL
HARK THE ARK
DEMENTED MENTOR
BECAUSE OF LOVE
MY BELOVED BOSS
THE ADAM BOMB
THE DROWNING FOOL
THE FRAGRANCE OF LOVE
GLORY DAYS
THE GOOD LIFE
A GOOD EXAMPLE OF A BAD DECISION
LOVE LETTERS
MIRROR IMAGE
THE MASTER PLAN-TER
NO GREATER LOVE
REALLY GOODBYE
HAVE FAITH LITTLE SEED
HOLY SPIRIT PLEASE
GOD ANSWERS PRAYER
THE PASSOVER LAMB
GOD'S THE BOSS

Gifts To The Giver ~The Early Years~

GIVER POEM IN THERE
RAINBOW OF DREAMS
TEMPUS FUGIT
SOUL GOAL
LET THE HEART SPEAK
ABBA WILL YOU HOLD ME?
BAA BAA ABBA
DO YOU KNOW THE TIME?
HELLUVA GAME
TREASURE OF A FRIEND
TAME YOUR TONGUE
GRANDPA'S EYES
THAT I MAY SEE
I LOVE YOU STILL
THE PRODIGAL
BECAUSE OF LOVE
THE KING'S TEARS
SISTERS
OH SOLOMON
I SEE GOD
SALVATION
STARGAZER
STELLAR RENDEZVOUS
THE FALL
GIMME THE GOOD LIFE
BLESS OUR LITTLE HOME
FIRE FIGHTERS

Monika Starr Langguth

~ 1 ~
OUR SON

Our Son was given to me by the Spirit of The Lord over 30 years ago. It was a very dark and sad time in my life. I was separated from my children due to a business decision which took me to New York and left my children in Florida attending school.

While my daughter was old enough and on her own sharing an apartment with a roommate, my son was only fifteen and too young to be away from his mother. Although, he was being cared for quite well, my heart was breaking that he was not with me. While I was working in New York, I took a weekend trip to see my children. When my son came over to my

daughter's apartment, he was the typical fourteen-year-old - happy to see me and excited to go with his sister to the mall. My heart was broken when I saw him. There was my son separated from his mother. All I could feel was guilt and extreme sadness.

I hurried off to the bathroom so that he would not see me in such distress. I locked the door and stood in the dark sobbing and feeling like a failure as a parent and a failure as a human being as well.

Rory, my son, and Monica, my daughter, called out that they were going and that they'd see me later. Usually, I would make sure that I kissed them goodbye, but I was so upset that I didn't want them to see me that way. So, I just answered from the bathroom that I'd see them later as well.

Gifts To The Giver ~ The Early Years ~

As the front door closed and they were gone, I totally broke down. Sobbing, I stood there in the total darkness... feeling as if I were suspended in time and space. Suddenly, I heard a voice. It was God! I immediately knew that it was God's voice because I was crying so bitterly that I felt no one could have reached me or comforted me at that moment.

"I want to speak with you." "Okay," I thought, I'm ready, "God, speak." "Get a piece of paper I want you to write this down." I threw open the door and wiping my eyes started running around the apartment looking for paper and a pen. This wasn't my house and I didn't have a clue where anything was. And then, in only the way God could do it, He said, "It's okay... I'll wait."

I was shaking uncontrollably, and my heart was beating almost out of my chest as Our Father Who Art in Heaven came to me through His Spirit and comforted one of His brokenhearted children. He still had time in His busy schedule of keeping all the planets in place and watching out for the billions of people on this earth to reach down and touch His child.

The attached poem was given to me by The Lord. It is just about how it was initially given except for about two stanzas which He gave to me later.

I pray that it blesses you as it has blessed me. In fact, over the years, this message has intensified because I have seen this promise in action. He is Our Father and we are His Children. That's all there is to it. May God touch your heart as you read His Message. I humbly admit that I am just the messenger. And for that I am honored.

This poem belongs to you, Dear Precious Child of God.
Be blessed and encouraged. The God of The Universe loves you.

Love in Jesus,
Monika Starr Langguth

Monika Starr Langguth

~ OUR SON ~

Oh, My Son, I Love You
Just to Look Upon Your Face
Fills My Heart with So Much Love
That Nothing Can Erase.
The Thought of Being Far from You
Is More Than I Can Bear.
For When I Need Your Special Touch,
I Shall Not Find Your There.
Soon My Mind Just Drifts Away
As Tears Then Fill My Eyes
In Fear That You Might Face "The Wolf"
Dressed in The Lamb's Disguise.

Yet, As I Mourn Within Myself,
I Hear That "Inner Voice" That Said,
"I Suffered Great Pains, Too,
Because I Made A Choice.
I Love My Son, My Holy Son
He's Shared All Life with Me.
He Has Been There Right by My Side
For All Eternity.
But, Then One Day, He Left My Side
Gave Up His Holy Throne,
To Live Amidst A Hating World.
My Jesus . . . All Alone.

Gifts To The Giver ~The Early Years~

If You Don't Think That Broke My Heart
Dear Child, Think Again.
I Gave the Firstborn of My Life
To Be Abused by Men.
The Night He Came into The World,
I Longed to Be the One
That Held Him and Rocked Him to Sleep
You See, That Was "My Son."
But If I Did Not Let Him Go
To Change Man's Destiny
There'd Just Be Angels, Jesus Christ,
The Holy Ghost and Me.

Well, Being the Father That I AM,
I Longed for All the Ones
That Would Become My Family
As My Daughters and My Sons.
Oh, To See Him Beaten! Mocked!
And Hung Upon A Tree!
That Thunder Was My Breaking Heart!
They Killed My Boy, You See!
To See Him Bleed and Watch Him Die
For All the Sins of Man
I Longed to Wipe All Mankind Out!
But Dared Not Lift My Hand

Monika Starr Langguth

Because Before He Bowed His Head,
I Heard My Loving Son,
"Father Forgive Them for What They Do.
Thy Know Not What They've Done!"
And Then the Worst Part of It All
Man's Sin Took Him to Hell.
All Heaven Cried, As Satan Laughed.
The Pain? Too Great to Tell.
Even Though with God, There Is No Time,
You Must Now See
That Losing Him for Three Full Days
Was Like... Eternity.

But, Oh, That Glorious Morning!
Behold! My Risen Son!
What Joy to See His Shining Face!
The Victory Was Won!
For Death Can't Keep "Life" In the Grave
He Died to Set Men Free.
And All Who Take Him for Their Lord
Then 'Death' They'll Never See.
Well, Now You Know Just How I Felt
And That I Promise You
That I Will Be Right by Your Son
You See, He's "My Son" Too."

Monika Starr Langguth
TGBTG
1996©

Gifts To The Giver ~ The Early Years ~

~ 2 ~
A READY WRITER

When The Lord gave me "Our Son" in 1986, it was the first time I had heard from God in such an intense way. Since I never thought He wouldn't speak with me or to me, I did not have any blocks to deter my spirit from hearing His. But, because I was extremely broken and needed so much healing and deliverance, it was not a very good connection. Like a radio that one cannot seem to tune in to the correct frequency, we either get a lot of static or hear stations crossing over each other. That's just like how the enemy operates. He seeks to talk over what we are trying to discern and since we have left all the windows open in our soul, all we can hear is the neighborhood of the "dark side" trying to override our thoughts.

I say this to bring you to what truly set me on this path as one who writes what I believe The Spirit of God is saying to me. It was not an overnight thing. It took a lot of discipline and humbling on my part to hear what The Spirit had to say. Just like the house with all the windows open and everyone yelling and blasting their boomboxes, I had to learn how to hear God and then listen long enough to grow and be delivered and healed. As I grew, I got the windows closed to the outside elements and learned to soundproof my soul. This takes time.

So, there I was; I was holding onto the "Our Son" message and reading that for dear life and for my children's lives as well. It was like a precious jewel you value and sometimes you'd open the vault and hold it and treasure it. But then what? What good was the jewel if it was just the only one you had? Was it helping or just becoming the object of your affection in some strange way?

Monika Starr Langguth

Would it be more useful if I cashed it in to benefit others rather than a coveted possession? I remember reading a saying, "An idea is dangerous if it's the only one you have." Soon, I became discontent with just this one message from God. I desired to have more of Him and wanted to write but only if that is what He wanted me to do. Was it just my own desire to write? Was there something else He wanted me to do? Was I stuck waiting for something to happen? I realize now that it was The Precious Holy Spirit prodding me to seek God for definition and direction.

So, this one Saturday night, June 20th, 1987, as I was getting ready for bed, I knelt on my bed and began to pray. "God do You want me to write? Is that what You want? I only want to do what You want me to do." Now imagine multiplying those questions about 100 times and add sobbing and crying and tears covering my entire body. Finally, after becoming completely exhausted and depleted of all the salt in my body via my eye ducts, I collapsed on my bed.

Suddenly I heard these words, "Yes, I have called you to be a writer." Jolting me back into consciousness, I immediately responded, "How do I know this is You?" Now, right about now, if I were God, I would have said, "Y'know, kid, you have been nagging Me for the last two hours, and now I answer you and you're questioning Who This is?" But, thankfully, God sees our frailty and responds with love and patience: "They will prophecy these very words over you tomorrow (at church)"

Sunday, June 21st, 1987. Talk about mental resurrection! I was pumped up! I don't remember how I slept that night, but rest assured, I was there ready and waiting, sitting in the front row to hear the thunderous, "Thus saith The Lord!!" In fact, I kept trying to get the pastor's attention, smiling at him and blinking my eyes. Thinking back on that now, I wonder if he thought I was flirting with him.

Gifts To The Giver ~ The Early Years ~

And then the service was over. "Okay, God bless everyone, see you next week," were the only prophetic words I heard from that dear man. I stood up in shock. All the joy and color drained from my face. What bothered me the most was not that I didn't receive a prophetic word, but that I was delusional . . . imagining that I heard from God. I walked to the back feeling worse than a bride left at the altar. With my head bowed down and my foot just about to cross the threshold, the pastor yelled out: "Monika, get up here! The Lord has a word for you!" Now I go from dejection to borderline horror. What is God going to say? Is He going to call me out for my arrogance and pride in thinking that "The God of Heaven" would talk to me? So down the aisle I walked as if I were on my way to the principal's office (something I remember too well) to be chastised big time.

We keep thinking God is like us. That's why He commanded, "Do not to make God in your own image." How we see ourselves or how we imagine Him to be. Imagination is creating images in the mind. We were made in His image, not the other way around. I found that out right then.

"I have anointed you with 'the tongue of a pen of a ready writer,' says The Lord ~ and it is to be used! No longer stifle My Spirit, but that anointing is to move forth in the power of My Spirit and your tongue is to flow and move as I speak it through you! Hold not shut what I seek to be opened, but be there as My mouthpiece, says The Lord, and be that tongue of a pen of a ready writer! So that which 'I will' shall be accomplished and that you will be a light to those in darkness. That they will be set free and My Word will go forth in power ~ cutting and breaking down and destroying darkness, says The Lord God."

What? is this a dream? "The tongue of a pen of a ready writer?" Anointed? Me? Isn't that for really important people? Those that never make mistakes?

Monika Starr Langguth

Back then, the prophecies were recorded and given to the receiver on a cassette.

I don't remember anything else about that day; I was floating around in another dimension. Did that really happen? I rushed home, put that cassette in the machine and played and played and played it.

You see, I was anointed!! Anointed!! Yes, anointed!! Honestly, I had no clue what anointed really meant. It was some big-time word used for the big-time people of God, but it sounded very impressive.

After playing the tape on what seemed like a continuous loop, I began to see it like the jewel in the vault. it was nice to hear but now what? So, I took a shot and asked God: "Okay, Lord, so when am I going to be famous?"

It's amazing how fast God can go from giving the baby the pacifier to a blast right between the eyes: "Well, what have you done?" Mortified, I felt if the universe was on the head of a pin, I was in there somewhere. Oh, so I had to do something? Duh, yeah!!

I humbly answered, "Um, well, um, nothing really"
"That's right so shut up and do something!"

I have told this story to people and one person was horrified. "God said, "Shut up?" Frankly, I wasn't shocked at all, I didn't need to hear the King James Version, "Shutteth uppeth!" I needed to hear it just like a girl from The Bronx needed to hear it, "Shut up!"
I shut up and did something. I began to write and put many of the things down that you will read. But, then, wanting to feed my pride and ego, I just had to hear that tape again; except I couldn't find it. So off I went to the Heavenly Complaint Department, "Lord, I can't find the tape." Immediately I heard The Holy Spirit, "What do you need it for? To puff yourself up? Do it!"

Gifts To The Giver ~ The Early Years ~

Man, this is getting rough! I feel like I'm in the military; but, I took it and just kept going. Looking back on all this, I am very thankful that: one, I had the guts to keep asking God, and two, that he was discipling me and "We" were getting down to business. "We" because this was His gig and He was

allowing me to be a part! I wanted to do this. I asked Him (or rather hounded Him) and He answered me and it was time "to do it!"

It seemed like over a year before I ever played that tape again. Pathetically, I did try to find it. Just like a kid sneaking around thinking that Mom doesn't see you stealing that cookie or pinching your brother, God saw me trying to pull a fast one. Like He didn't know! Yeah, right!

So, after not being able to find it on my own, I finally broke down and asked The Lord in the sweetest little voice I could muster; just like a kid trying to get the desired result. The only thing missing was, "Pretty please with sugar on top?" "Look in that basket." Since I had gone through that wicker basket that held my cassettes maybe twenty times. I thought, "Oh, now I've got Him!" I guess He didn't know I looked in that basket. I had a lot to learn about God, didn't I? So, I looked in the basket, as I was running my mouth, "Oh, Lord, do You know how many times I've looked in this thing? I'm telling You, it's not . . ." and while making a total fool of myself, I pulled out the cassette. It was the first one!! Again, just like The Lord, He wasn't wasting time berating me as I would have done if the tables were reversed and my kid gave me so much lip. He knew that I knew He knew. I played the cassette. When it finished, I heard Holy Spirit ask, "It doesn't seem the same, does it?" "No, Lord, it doesn't." He so lovingly replied, "That is because it's not just a dream or a promise, it's become a reality." And dear reader, I never played it again.

There's a little "P.S." to this. Although I did not play the tape again and in fact, I don't recall ever seeing it again, I did remind The Lord of what He had said to me. I used to think it was borderline nagging Him, but now I have come to understand that when we bring what He said to remembrance, we confirm that we trust Him. We also remind ourselves that what He said will come to pass if we trust Him and keep going. I have said for a very long time, "We work our entire life to become an overnight success." If God is patient with us, then we too, must trust the process. So, just keep going dear friend!

~3~
BEAUTY ETERNAL

One day, the Apostles Peter and John went to the Temple one afternoon to take part in the three o'clock prayer service. As they approached the Temple, a man lame from birth was being carried in. Each day he was put beside the Temple gate, the one called the "Beautiful Gate," so he could beg from the people going into the Temple. When he saw Peter and John about to enter, he asked them for some money.

Peter and John looked at him intently, and Peter said, "Look at us!" The lame man looked at them eagerly, expecting some money. But Peter said, "I don't have any silver or gold for you. But I'll give you what I have. In the name of Jesus Christ, the Nazarene, get up and walk!"

Then Peter took the lame man by the right hand and helped him up. And as he did, the man's feet and ankles were instantly healed and strengthened. He jumped up, stood on his feet, and began to walk! Then, walking, leaping, and praising God, he went into the Temple with them.
I gave a Beauty Seminar and wrote this for the ladies.

Monika Starr Langguth

BEAUTY ETERNAL

Oh, Beauty! Beauty! Fleeting Thing...
You Light A While... Then Take Wing
　To Find A Younger Resting Place
　Of Smoother Skin and Fairer Face.

But, In God's Word We Have Been Told
　That Beautiful We Can Behold
　And Not Just Beg Outside the Gate
　And Plead for Alms till It's Too Late.

Though Some May Have Silver and Gold
　They Can't Forever Beauty Hold.

　Yet, If We Close Our Carnal Eyes
　And Seek Where "Beauty" Truly Lies
　And Ask God That the World May See
　The Beauty of Whom Dwells in Thee.

Then Through Our Lips, Those Lost Will Hear It
　That Living in Us Is "The Spirit"
　Now Beautiful... Each Person Sees Us
　For Shining Through Us Is Christ Jesus.

Gifts To The Giver ~The Early Years~

No Longer At "Gate" Beautiful
Arise! Into the Temple... Dwell!

Monika Starr Langguth
TGBTG
1989©

Monika Starr Langguth

~4~
BE NOT SLEEPING

One Night When I And Slumber Met
I Dreamt About The Lord
And There in Glory 'Round His Throne
We Worshiped and Adored.
Yet, as I Looked into His Face
That Shone Bright as The Sun,
Dare I To Think That in Those Eyes
Are Tears, Most Holy One?

It's Over, Lord, We're Home at Last
No Longer Will We Stray
But I Could See His Heart Was Cast
So Very Far Away.
And Then for Just A Lightning Flash
I Saw Why He Should Weep
For This Good Shepherd Loves His Flock
And Mourns A Loss of Sheep.

Then Tears Like Diamonds Streamed His Face
And as They Dropped . . . They Burned
As If Those Sheep to Be His Jewels
Would Never More Return.
I Then Looked Back into My Life
And I, One of The Flock
Remembered Some of Those Poor Sheep
That Fell Upon the Rocks.

Gifts To The Giver ~The Early Years~

Perhaps, If I Had Helped Them Back
To Safety with The Others
They'd Be in Heaven Right Now
With My Sisters and My Brothers.
Yet, As I Saw Them Start to Roam
And Wander from The Rest
I Did Not Call to Them at All
I Sadly Must Confess.

Oh, Lord, I Am So Sorry
That I Didn't Care Enough
To Help My Brother When He Fell
And Life for Him Got Tough.
If Only I Had Helped Just One
That's One Less Tear You'd Cry.
Lord, If I Had Another Chance...
"You Do!" Was His Reply.

When Sheepishly I Looked Again
I Woke to Find That All
That I Had Dreamed Would Someday Be
Unless I Heed the Call.
For If I Truly Love You, Lord,
I Don't Want You to Weep
I'll Do as You've Commanded
I'll Go and Feed Your Sheep.

Monika Starr Langguth
TGBTG
1988©

Monika Starr Langguth

~ 5 ~
THANK YOU, FATHER, FOR MY MOTHER

Oh, Dear Father Up Above
Forever Showing of Your Love
Who Sent Your Son to Be My Brother
Sent Love Again . . . In Form of Mother.

In All Ways Showing That You Care
When I Was Born You Placed Her There
To Love Me and To Care for Me
Until I Returned Back to Thee.

And by The Love She Made Me Feel
I Could Believe Your Love Was Real.
She Taught Me That True Joy in Life
Was Living It in Jesus Christ.

And That the Reason We're on Earth
Is to Live on Through Second Birth.
To Share with All, The Truth We've Heard
By Living And Speaking Your Word

Then When My Life Down Here Is Through,
She Said I Would Go Back to You
Where Never More We'd Pain or Cry
And We Would Never Say "Goodbye."

Gifts To The Giver ~The Early Years~

How Blessed to Think That Little Me
Was Thought So Valuable to Thee
You'd Send The Christ To Be My Brother
And Then to Send to Me ... A Mother!!

Monika Starr Langguth
TGBTG
Mother's Day 1990 ©

~ 6 ~
ONE DAY IN HEAVEN

On July 14th, of 2000, on a Friday, I was listening to the Christian Radio Station and the scripture of the day was Jeremiah 33:3 - "Call unto Me and I will answer you and tell you great and mighty things which you do not know." I usually do not listen to the radio (but Cd's) and so this was most unusual. The entire time, the radio announcer kept repeating the scripture Jeremiah 33:3. In fact, my entire ride to work of 45 minutes and back that evening, the radio host kept reminding me of that scripture.

Due to a series of heartbreaking events, I was not with my Mother and did not know that she was ailing and dying in a hospital. No one in my family called to tell me. Sadly, it was the deliberate decision of my siblings not notify me of my Mother's failing health. What was so hurtful was that I took care of my Mother for many years, and her second husband with Alzheimer's disease . . . so to be treated with such cruelty was painful.

Later that very day, at 9:30 pm a friend of mine called to tell me that my brother had called, asking him (friend) to relay the message that my Mother had died that very day at 12:30 noon. It was now 9:30 at night. Of course, I cried myself to sleep, and upon awakening in the morning, I sat up and immediately remembered that my Mother had died.

The first thing I said when I awoke was, "Oh, Mom, it's your first day in Heaven." As I sat on the edge of my bed, The Precious Holy Spirit reminded me of the scripture verse from the day before. I heard in my heart

"Jeremiah 33:3" Sobbing, I replied, "Jeremiah 33:3 ~ Call unto me and I will answer you and tell you great and mighty things which you do not know."

Gifts To The Giver ~ The Early Years ~

Then I heard That Beautiful Voice speak to my heart again, "Call unto me and ask me." I said, "Oh, Lord, tell me something I do not know."

Immediately, I was swept up into a vision where I saw my mother. Although she was 89 when she died, in the vision she was very young and beautiful and looked like I remembered her when I was a very little child. It amazed me because I did not even remember that she looked like that until I saw her in the vision and it jolted my memory back to a time I had forgotten. My Mother seemed to be floating yet standing straight as if in suspension. She was wearing an airy white gossamer gown while floating inside the most beautiful whirlwind of dazzling sparkling prismatic diamond dust. The dust was so filled with light that it was like billions of teeny diamonds whirling and swirling around her at what appeared to be at distance of about eight feet away from where she was centered. In this glorious vision, I saw faces of people who seemed to be coming forth out of the whirlwind and softly calling her name, "Catherine, Catherine!" Then they would go back into the whirlwind and another person's face would appear and call her name. My Mother reacted just like someone would who had just come into a "Surprise Party" where she was the guest of honor and as she scanned the room, she saw all the people who were there to help her celebrate; overjoyed and thrilled as they called her name. Slowly and gracefully she was turning in the whirlwind, lovingly being greeted by all those friends and relatives that had gone to Heaven before her. It was funny ~ I recognized all the people calling out to her even though I had never seen them or known them on earth. I knew that God had heightened my spiritual awareness to see and understand what I was looking at.

After about a minute of watching this magnificent vision, I heard The Lord say, "Get up and write what you see." I answered, "I can't leave this." He spoke again, "Get up and write or you will never remember this." I immediately got up and as I sat at the computer, The Holy Spirit took over the keyboard and using my fingers, the following message was created.

Monika Starr Langguth

Since My Mother's passing was in 2000, it is many years since that vision and I must tell you, I still remember it as clearly as I did the day that The Lord blessed me with that magnificent experience.

The Holy Spirit whispered to my heart, "You see they only saw your Mother as she died... but I show you, your Mother alive!" God in His infinite love and mercy was not going to let me be robbed of being a part of my Mother's life or spend years wrestling with what would have never given me peace or closure. What could have been a very long time of mourning over the loss of my Mother was turned into a blessing and everlasting thanks to my God Who showed me my Mother whole and beautiful and living in Eternal Life.

My prayer is that you are blessed by the message and that if you have lost a loved one, or are fearing the coming end of someone's life, that you let this message resonate in your heart.

If the one you love is a Child of God, saved by the Blood of Jesus Christ, then he or she will be living in eternal bliss and wholeness and waiting for you in that Glorious Land, Our True Home, called Heaven.

God Bless You.

Monika Starr Langguth
TGBTG
7-15-2000 ©

Gifts To The Giver ~The Early Years~

ONE DAY IN HEAVEN

Though You're Just One Day in Heaven
Is it like a Million Years
Since You've Remembered All Your Pains
And All Those Worldly Tears?

Was it Faster than a Lightning Flash
And You Were in the Gaze
Of the Precious Rose of Sharon
And the Ancient of All Days?

Is the Glory of His Presence
Like a Light You've Never Known?
Has He Walked You in His Gardens?
Let You Sit Beside His Throne?

He Has Whispered to My Very Heart
That Everyone Is There
That Once from You Had to Depart
But Now Forever Share.

He Has Shown Me That Your Smile
Is Quite Different than Before
That Which Lasted Just A While
Now Will Be Forevermore.

Monika Starr Langguth

Surrounded by Your Loved Ones.
Oh, They Are a Happy Crowd.
Radiating His Pure Essence
In a Great Prismatic Cloud.

Love and Peace and Joy and Praise
Shines Forth from Everyone
Reflecting Very Light, Himself.
The "One and Only One."

How Can I Grieve for You, My Love?
Though Apart We Now Must Be.
For You Have Reached True Home Above
Where You Now Wait for Me.

Monika Starr Langguth
TGBTG
7-15-2000©

Gifts To The Giver ~The Early Years~

The Divine Editor is at it again.

There is a prelude to this happening. About a month before My Mother died, I had visited her in a hospital in Memphis Tennessee. When she was moved to a nursing home, I was not allowed to know where she was staying. I called and after asking and asking, I saw that I was not going to get an answer.

I hung up the phone and screamed, "I hate them!" I was referring to my brothers and sister. Immediately I saw The Lord in the corner of my room and a large spear shot into His center and He doubled over as He was deeply wounded. I was horrified at that vision and cried out, "Oh, Lord, forgive me. Forgive me for my words. I forgive them as no one is worth my hurting you." I saw right then how pained He is when we hold anything against another. Even if they have wronged us.

As I was preparing for this book, Holy Spirit said to me, "Had you not forgiven those that had offended you and kept you from your Mother, then I would not have shared this vision with you. Your obedience to forgive touched God's heart to bless you."

Forgiveness is worth it.

Monika Starr Langguth

~ 7 ~
DADDY'S LITTLE GIRL

Dear Lord, Sometimes I Feel So Sad
My Little Girl Has Had No "Dad"
The One She Could Say, "Daddy" To
And in Hard Times, Would See Her Through.
How Could Life Be So Very Cruel
To Not Appreciate This Jewel?
I Can't Believe He'd Never Bother
To Love Her and To Be Her "Father."
And as The Tears Streamed Down My Face
I Felt God's Presence in That Place
And All the Things Man Can Destroy
Were Filled with Love and Peace and Joy.

"My Child, What You Say Is True
And I Know How You're Feeling, Too.
For I, Too, Loved A Special One
He Is Your Lord... He Is My Son.
I Found It So Sad to Conceive
That What He Said, They'd Not Believe.
Yet, Chose the Wicked Evil Force
And Nailed My Child to The Cross.
But I AM God... I'm Not A Fool
And I Will Judge Those That Are Cruel.
I'll Judge Them for They Have Defiled
Life's Greatest Gift... A Little Child.
Do Not Cry for Your Little Girl

Gifts To The Giver ~The Early Years~

For in My Eyes, She Is A Pearl
That I Hold Deep Within My Heart
And Never from Her, I'll Depart
Because She Took My Son to Be
Her Savior for Eternity.
Now She Is Grafted in The Vine
And Part of Heaven's Royal Line.
I've Watched Her as She's Grown in Grace
In Spirit... And So Fair of Face.
I AM The One If She Should Weep
Who Gently Lulls Her Off to Sleep.

I Love Her More Than You Can Know
I Sent My Son to Tell Her So.
With His Blood My Son Has Bought Her
Now She Is More Mine Than Your Daughter.
Do Not Shed Tears for Man to Love
Her True Father Is Here Above.
Now Be at Peace... I Promise You
This "Daddy's" Love... Forever True.

Monika Langguth
TGBTG
1993©

Monika Starr Langguth

~ 8 ~
# HARK THE ARK

Right till The End When the Rains Came Down
They Were Living It Up and Painting the Town.
They Were Craving for Life and All Fleshly Desire.
Take A Pretty Big Rain to Put Out That Fire.

Old Noah... He Tried to Tell Them the Story
Too High A Price to Give Up Self-Glory
So, They Lusted and Danced Like Perverted Trains
As They Mocked the Sprinkling of Heavenly Rains.

As Each Adulterer, Thief and Liar
Danced Round and Round, The Rains Got Higher
Yet, On They Went in Their Sin-Filled Haste
Caring Not That the Waters Had Reached Their Waist.

They Just Rushed to Party on Higher Ground
While the Rains Continued to Pour Right Down
By Now, The Water Was to Their Chins
Soon the People Would Perish - Drown in Their Sins.

The Earth in Flood... The Sky Grew Dark
"We've Changed Our Minds! Let Us on The Ark!"
But the Door Was Closed and The Ark Took Sail
People Screamed and Died... You Could Hear Them Wail!

Gifts To The Giver ~The Early Years~

For They Wanted to Do What They Wanted to Do
Caring Not to Believe That God's Word Is True!
You've Heard the Story... It's Time My Friend
To Decide If You Follow God... Or Men.

You Must Be Ready... No Time to Wait
When the Door Is Closed... It's Just Too Late
Take A Good Hard Look at The People's Ways
They're No Different Now Than in Noah's Days.

They're All Living It Up and Painting the Town
Double-Daring God to Let The "Rains" Come Down
God Will Never Again Destroy Man by Flood
He Who Lives for Self... Drowns in His Own Blood.

We Can Live for God... And Make the Right Choice
Or Party So Loud, We Can't Hear His Voice.
Swim in Sin... You'll Drown in Eternal Death
A Real Long Time to Try to Hold Your Breath.

Life's Got Its "Rains" but My Friend, You'll See
There's A Greater Plan for You and Me
God Said to The World, "My Son - I'll Send!"
And His Treasure's Forever at The Rainbow's End.

Where to Spend Eternity? You Get to Choose.
If Your Choice Ain't Jesus... Guess What? You Lose!

Monika Langguth
TGBTG
1991©

Monika Starr Langguth

~ 9 ~
DEMENTED MENTOR

Come Blinded Ones, Before Me Sit
And Listen to Prince Counterfeit
I Want Your Soul – Yes! All of It.

Keep Up the Work, My Little Tools
And While Your Fingers Dangle Jewels
You've Dealt Yourselves the Hand of Fools.

No Fear! No Fear! I Am Not Here
I Whisper Softly in Your Ear
The Truth I Twist So Crystal Clear

I Love the Fact That You Insist
That I Simply Do Not Exist
So, In Your Bondage, I Persist

Disguised... I Purr Like Angel's Wings
Beneath the Whirr... I Pull Your Strings.
Such Ecstasy Destruction Brings.

I Send to You - Your "Inner Guide"
He Makes You Feel as God Inside
Better Known - His Name Is Pride.

Gifts To The Giver ~The Early Years~

Go! Covet All That You Desire!
For There Is No "Eternal Fire!"
But, Then Again... I Am "The Liar"

I Reign as "Prince of Blasphemy"
Yet, It Is Written... "Doom for Me!"
Yessss... Misery Loves Company.

Monika Starr Langguth
1995©
TGBTG

Monika Starr Langguth

~ 10 ~
BECAUSE OF LOVE

It's Just Because I Love You
That I Feel We'll Part Someday
And I Will Go to Heaven
And You'll Go "Another Way"

Many Nights I Lay Awake
And Find It Hard to Sleep
Or Walk into Another Room
So You Won't See Me Weep.

As Long as I Have Known You
I Have Loved You … That Is True
And Never Want to Be the Cause
Of Bringing Pain to You

But I Feel You Get So Angry
When I Tell You of My King
That You Resent the Joy I Have
That Lifts My Heart to Sing.

It's Because The Father Loved Us
That He Sent His Son to Earth
To Ransom Back "His Stolen Ones"
(To God, We Have Great Worth.)

Gifts To The Giver ~The Early Years~

Because You Mean So Much to Me
And I Say This from My Heart
I Fear That in The Future
You and I Will Someday Part.

I Want to Share Eternal Life with You
And Leave You Never
For Jesus Promises, "In Him"
That We Can Live Forever!

It's A Sad Thing I Must Tell You
And to Say This Makes Me Cry
But, If Jesus Christ Is Not Your Lord,
Then Someday, We'll Say, "Goodbye."

Monika Starr Langguth
TGBTG
1995©

Monika Starr Langguth

~ 11 ~
MY BELOVED BOSS

Oh, How Much I Want
To Do The Lord's Work...
But, More Times Than Not
I'm A Spiritual Jerk.

Anyone Else
Would Surely Have Fired Me
Every Time I Repent
He Always Rehires Me.

Monika Starr Langguth
TGBTG
1995©

Gifts To The Giver ~The Early Years~

~ 12 ~
THE ADAM BOMB

I Am Adam
Not as In Atom Bomb
But... You Might Say, As Adam... I Bombed.
I Pried the Lid Off "Life"
That Part Of "Life" That Leads to Death.

That's A Good Reason to Hate Me...
I Was Weak
Have You Ever Been Weak?
Even Though I Was the Founder of The Adam Bomb...
That's Not the End of The Story.

God Sent to Earth A Scud Missile
That Puts an End to The Adam Bomb...
If You, My Descendants,
Will Allow That Scud Missile into Your Life.

Jesus Christ Is That Scud Missile.
By the Way, Adam Means "Man".
Jesus Christ Is Known as The Second Adam
But Really Is the Last Adam.

Monika Starr Langguth

So, Take It from Someone Who Knows. . .
The Worst Mistake Someone Can Make
Is Rejecting God. . .
I Know . . . I Did.

And Because of My Big Mistake,
My Descendants Have Been Paying for It Ever Since . . .
But God Made A Way

He's So Wonderful
That He Is Not Making You Pay for My Mistake.
He Sent Jesus And If You Accept Him . . .
You Would No Longer Be Part of The Adam Bomb.

On the Other Hand,
If You Don't Accept Him,
Then You, My Friend,
Have Made Your Own Adam Bomb
And Someday It's Gonna Blow You Clear to Hell.

Monika Starr Langguth
TGBTG
1990©

Gifts To The Giver ~ The Early Years ~

~ 13 ~
THE DROWNING FOOL

A Man Blinded by His Own Choice
Had Closed His Heart to Hear Truth's Voice
And Heeding Not the Warning Knocks,
Sailed His Life-Ship into The Rocks.

The Man and Boat Were Both Tri-Hull
The Man Was Spirit, Body, Soul
The Boat's Tri-Parts Then Cracked and Sank
Both Man and Boat the Sea Soon Drank.

The Ship Would Not Have Sailed Off Course
Had Man Let God Be His Life Force
And So, The Vessel Died That Day
Because the Man Had Sailed His Way

But, Look Again... For the Man Still
Swims Despite the Ocean's Chill!
Yet, Through His Watered Chokes, He Sputters:
"It's Your Fault, God!" He Scorns and Mutters

Still, God Puts Out His Hand to Save
The Blinded Fool... The Drowning Knave
And as The Man Goes Down Once More,
He Cries with Wrath Just Like Before:

Monika Starr Langguth

"I'll Save Myself! Remove Your Hand!
I Don't Need You to Reach Dry Land!"
And God Respects the Fool's Last Wish
And Lets Him Sink Among the Fish.

But, Even from The Ocean's Depths
God Listens for The Man's Last Breath
To Cry, "God Save Me from Myself!"
The Savior Waits... Just Cry for Help.

Monika Starr Langguth
TGBTG
1990©

~ 14 ~
THE FRAGRANCE OF LOVE

The Mind Cannot Explain
The Fragrance of a Rose
And God, Not to The Intellect
But to The Humble … Shows.

Those That Flaunt Brilliant Recall
Deceived Within Their Art
For God Already Knows It All …
He's Beckoned by The Heart

Monika Starr Langguth
TGBTG
1990 ©

Monika Starr Langguth

~ 15 ~
GLORY DAYS

Oh, Lord, Let These Eyes
See Myself in Paradise!
Let These Weary Feet
Walk the Golden Street!

Let This Trembling Hand
Touch the Promised Land!
Let These Quivering Lips
My Sweet Savior Kiss!

Never More to Roam
Father, I'll Be Home!

We Will Drink and Sup
Share The Master's Cup!
Dance and Sing and Praise
Happy All the Days!

Never More to Die
Joyful Spirits Cry!
This Is All for Us
When We Love Jesus!!!!

Monika Starr Langguth
TGBTG ~ 1988 ©

Gifts To The Giver ~ The Early Years ~

~ 16 ~
THE GOOD LIFE

"Yeah! Gimme The Good Life . . . So Much and So Often!"
Then It Waves You 'Goodbye' As Your Placed in Your Coffin.

All the Things That You Gotta Have Now
When You're Breathing Your Last, Don't Help You Somehow.
They're Left in The Corner for Someone to Sell
In Exchange for The Ticket That Takes You to Hell.

"I Gotta Look Good! Admired! Adored!"
The "Got" That You Should Got, Ya Don't Got . . . "The Lord!"
Don't Tell Me 'Bout Jesus! Cause I Don't Give A Damn, Sir!
But, Damned Is What's Left! Cause That Man Is the Answer.

He Isn't All Glitz . . . Or Muscles . . . Or Jewels
But The "Forever Treasure" Rejected by Fools.
Without Him, You'll Face Death at The Threshold
With Him, You Conquer the Power That Flesh Holds.

You Say That the Meaning of Life's to Be Lavished
Your Eyes Tell the Truth . . . In Your Soul, You Are Ravaged
God's Promise Is Solid . . . Just Try Him, You'll See
His Love Surpasses the Depths of The Sea

Your Eyes Will See Truth . . . And Your Heart Will Hear It
As You Soar in The Realm of The Eternal Spirit.
For God Is Forever . . . He Lives by No Clock
His Foundation Is Firm . . . So, Stand on This Rock.

Monika Starr Langguth

He Says He Has Gone to A "Place" We Can Be
"I've Built You A Mansion... Now Come Follow Me."
Jesus Now Stands at Your Heart-Door... And Knocks.
Dear Friend, It's Too Late When You're Placed in The Box.

Monika Starr Langguth
TGBTG ~ 1988©

Gifts To The Giver ~ The Early Years ~

~ 17 ~
A GOOD EXAMPLE OF A VERY BAD DECISION

Judas Was One of The Twelve
There in The Upper Room.
Yet, After Supping with The Lord
Went Out to Seal HIS Doom.

"Go and Do It Quickly"
Jesus Whispered 'Neath His Breath
And Judas ... For Some Silver
Sold The Savior into Death.

Although He and The Master
Walked and Talked Most Every Day
God's "Kingdom Come" Was Good for Some.
He Wanted His ... Today!

Crucified Upon A Cross
And Laid Within A Tomb
Three Days Later ... Jesus Rose!
Earth Birthed Him from Her Womb.

Now Jesus Lives Forevermore!
And All Who Know Him, Too.
But You Can Choose Christ ... Or Refuse
He Leaves That Up to You.

Monika Starr Langguth

Well... Judas Went and Hung Himself
A "Cursed Field" Where He Fell
He Chose "The Master of Disaster"
Whose "Kingdom Come" Is Hell.

Monika Langguth
TGBTG
1988©

Gifts To The Giver ~ The Early Years ~

~ 18 ~
LOVE LETTERS

Lord, It Seems Like Forever
Since I've Written A Letter to You.
To Thank You for How Much You Love Me
I Feel It in All That I Do.

I Can Look at A Problem Before Me
Then I Reach Out to You in A Prayer
The Spirit Is There Softly Guiding
Soon the Problem Is No Longer There

As I Sit in My Room All Alone
Just the Beat of The Clock and My Heart
I Know That You're Right There Beside Me
(As You've Always Been Right from The Start.)

Sometimes in A Dream, I Get Frightened
And I Cry Out for You in My Sleep
You Hold Up Your Staff to Protect Me
The Good Shepherd Takes Care of His Sheep.

You Fill Me with Love Overflowing
I Long for The Day When We'll Meet
Face to Face with The Very Love of My Life
As I Place Glory's Crown at Your Feet.

Monika Starr Langguth

Your Countenance So Overwhelming
Your Voice Will Be Tender and Mild
You'll Lift Me Up into Your Great Arms and Say,
"You've Come Home at Last, My Dear Child!"

But, Lord, Till the Day That It Happens
When My Greatest of Dreams Has Come True
I'll Lie on My Bed with A Pen in My Hand
And Write My Love Letters to You.

Monika Starr Langguth
TGBTG
1990 ©

~ 19 ~
MIRROR IMAGE
(To An Aging Mother)

Dear Mother, As I Look at You
I See the Child You Once Knew
And When I Hold You in My Arms
I Long to Keep You from All Harms.

Yet as We Go and Sing Life's Song
You Now Are Weak, and I Am Strong
But Only Weak Within the Shell
For in You, "All That's Living" Dwells.

Somehow, I Feel That I Am Cursed
That Now Our Lives Have Been Reversed
And One Day You Will Breathe A Breath
That Enters into What's Called "Death"

But, Death to Us Is Not the Night
In Death, We Enter Into "Light"
And Shine Before the Holy One
Where There Is Never Need of Sun.

Monika Starr Langguth

And as You Shed Your Hair of Gray
A Crown of Gold the Lord Will Lay
Upon Your Head and You Will Gleam
Like You've Awakened from A Dream

Of Tears and Sorrow, Pain and Strife
To Truly Enter Into "Life"
So, If You Go Within A While
Deep Down My Spirit Has to Smile
Although Your Face I Cannot Kiss
And Your Sweet Voice I'll Truly Miss

From Me, You Never Will Depart
For You Now Dwell in Heaven's Heart.
And Jesus Promised We Shall Be
Together for Eternity.

I Promise That I Will Not Mourn
For You Await My Coming Dawn
When I Will Leave All Worldly Harms
And You Will Hold Me in Your Arms . . . Again.

Monika Starr Langguth
TGBTG
1990©

~ 20 ~
THE MASTER PLAN-TER

Let The Holy Spirit Do His Job Today
Let Our Spirits Hear It and Simply... Obey!

In the Realm of God's Will, Ask Him What's Our Part?
Simple! Sow The Word's Seed in Your Heart... And Start!

Water It Now Daily with The Word Again
Soon Your Fruits Will Spring Up Before God and Men.

Cultivate Your Fruits Now with The Word Some More
Then You'll Reap A Harvest You've Not Seen Before.

Sowing Is Not Easy... You'll Get Cuts and Scars
Let The Spirit Do His Job... And We Do Ours.

Take God's Will for Your Life... Sprinkle It Around
Then You'll See What God Grows Given "Holy Ground."

Monika Starr Langguth
TGBTG
1990©

Monika Starr Langguth

~ 21 ~
NO GREATER LOVE

I Only Wish I Loved You, Lord,
The Way That You Love Me.
That I Would Stand for What I Am
And Have Become Through Thee.

And Though I Hung Not on A Cross
As You Have Done for Me,
I Must Stand at The Crossroads Now
For All the World to See.

For All the Whips You Took for Me
And How You Bled and Died
I Must Lay Down My "Inner Man"
Till Self Is Crucified.

For It Is Not till I Feel Death
And All My Life I Give
That I Will Conquer Death Through You
And in You… Truly Live.

Monika Starr Langguth
TGBTG
1990©

~ 22 ~
REALLY GOODBYE

"Come On! Let's Get Drunk Tonight!
Let's Go Hit Some Bars!
I've Been Itching' For A Fight
Hand Out A Few Scars."

"No," I Said, "I Don't Think So
I've Got Things to Do."
"Man!" My Friend Said, "I Don't Know
What's Got into You!

Ever Since You Went That Night
To Hear That Preacher Speak
Don't You Know That God's a Crutch
For Cowards and The Weak?"

Then He Pointed to My Bible
Looked at Me and Said,
"Only Time That I'll Hold That
Is in My Casket... Dead!"

"When You're Dead... It's Just Too Late!"
He Laughed... He Wouldn't Hear It
His Decision Sealed His Fate
I Felt It in My Spirit.

Monika Starr Langguth

"See You 'Round, Old Bible Man,
But It Won't Be Often
Gotta Party While You Can!
Soon You're in Your Coffin!"

Then He Bolted Out the Door
That Was His "Goodbye"
Something I'd Not Felt Before
Made Me Want to Cry.

I Stood Staring at The Wall
Numb... Like I Was Frozen
A Voice Then Said, "Many Are Called
Just So Few Are Chosen

My Heart Longs for All to Be
Part of My Great Plan
The Choice They Make Is Not by Me.
Free Will I Gave to Man

Blinded by His Pride and Sin
He Can't See The Light
He Will Never Let Me In
He Will Die... Tonight."

Early That Next Morning
A Phone Call Came to Me
Death Gave Him No Warning
When He Hit That Tree.

Gifts To The Giver ~The Early Years~

In the Casket, He Laid Dead
A Bible in His Hand
Never Caring That It Said,
"God Has A Master Plan."

Well, They Buried My Old Friend
It Hit Me Kind of Hard
His End Really Was "The End"
He Said, "No!" To God.

Eternity's Too High A Stake
To Put Off Knowing Jesus
Salvation's Plan Is for Our Sake
It Breaks Death's Chains… And Frees Us.

Monika Starr Langguth
TGBTG
1988©

Monika Starr Langguth

~ 23 ~
HAVE FAITH LITTLE SEED

Something Has Ended ... A Death as It Seems
Perhaps in Your Plans ... In Your Hopes ... In Your Dreams
But They Are Just Sleeping A While ... I Have Found
Christ Promises Nothing Will Stay Underground.

The Light of His Glory Will Cause Things to Rise
Things Thought to be Dead Will Live Before Your Eyes
Not as They Once Were ... Much Different Indeed
When God Is The Planter and We Are the Seed.

Just as The Seed Finds It Dark 'Neath The Earth
If We Wait on Him ... Soon the Seed Will Give Birth
And What Seemed So Empty ... So Lost ... And So Broken
Will Be Overflowing When God's Word Is Spoken.

Although We Have Fruit ... We Need Seeds to Grow More
So, Seed, Wait in Darkness ... God Has More in Store.
And Stand on His Promise ... In His Perfect Hour
Breaking Through the Darkness Your Faith Seed Will Flower.

Straight for His Light, Your Blessed Spirit Will Shoot
And You'll Have Abundance ... For God Grows "Good Fruit."

Monika Starr Langguth
TGBTG
1995©

~ 24 ~
HOLY SPIRIT...PLEASE!!!

Holy Spirit, Please Convict Me
When I Say, "Ho Hum...Oh, Well."
And I Watch as Men Go Blindly
Marching Off en route to Hell.

Please Don't Let Me Rest A Moment
In My Spiritual Bulls-Eye
Now That I Have Reached The "Target"
So Complacent as They Die.

Holy Spirit, I Beseech You
Never Let Me Have A Day
When I Worry Not That Someone
Doesn't Know Christ Is "The Way."

Oh, Great Comforter and Teacher
Never Let Me Lose the Sight
That I, Too, Was Once a Blindman
Till You Brought Me to The Light.

Monika Starr Langguth

Oh, Sweet Spirit of The Triune
Make Me Long to Tell All Men
Praying That It Burns Within Them
And They Pray This Prayer Again.

Monika Starr Langguth
TGBTG
1990©

Gifts To The Giver ~The Early Years~

~25~
GOD ANSWERS PRAYER

I Placed My Hands Together
And Prayed That God Would Bless Me
And as The Tears Fell from My Eyes
The Spirit Did Caress Me.

And in The Months That Followed
With My Hand, I Now Could Feel
The Little Life Stirring Inside
My "Blessing" Now Was Real.

Then Came the Day That They Would Place
My Blessing Small and Grand
Into My Arms and I Would Hold
That Small and Tender Hand.

The Years Moved On ... And So Did We
And Life Was Still So Sweet
That Little Hand Clutched Inside Mine
As We Would Cross the Street.

Those Growing Hands Soon Worked Controls
And Gadgets with Such Ease
And Stretched Them Out ... So Sure, No Doubt
I'd Give Up the Car Keys.

Monika Starr Langguth

But Like the Wind That Blows the Clouds
The Years Went Swiftly By
And Those Grown Hands... Off to New Lands
Would Sadly Wave "Goodbye."

Still, I Can Go Back in My Heart
Where Nothing Ever Pales
And See That Precious Little Hand
With Fine and Tiny Nails.

And So, In Prayer... These Old Hands Now
Ask God Again to Bless
My Life This Time... A Different Way
And His Answer Was, "Yes."

And Now Today Through Glistening Eyes
A Gift Like Nothing Other
This Hand I Hold... One Hour Old
Has Made Me A Grandmother.

With Love I Gaze Upon These Hands
With Fine and Tiny Nails
And Know Within My Heart of Hearts
That Our God Never Fails.

Lord, As This Little One Soon Grows
I Pray That I'll Be There
To Place Those Little Hands in Mine
And Teach:
"God Answers Prayer."

Monika Starr Langguth
TGBTG ~ 1990©

~ 26 ~
THE PASSOVER LAMB

A Monument of Self Was There
Of Flesh and Bone and Teeth and Hair.
In 'Sea of Me' I Chose to Swim
Deciding Best Let No One In.

As Time Went On, I Roamed the Halls
Of Self-Indulgent Iron Walls
And Made Quite Sure Without A Doubt
Let No One In and Nothing Out.

Yet as The Clock in Circled Flight
Abandoned Youth to Present Night
Illusions Now Were Not So Grand
I'd Built My Kingdom Upon Sand.

For Now, My Springtime Had Gone Passed
A Wintered Soul Reflects the Glass
A Crumbling Tower of Despair
Of Flesh and Bone and Teeth and Hair.

Awaiting Death . . . I Chose to Mourn
Then Heard A Dove Praising the Dawn
That Sang About A "Risen Son"
That's Shining Still When Day Is Done.

Monika Starr Langguth

Could This Be True? Once Thought Absurd?
I Felt His Heartbeat in His Word.
His Brilliance Made My Darkness Worse.
I Sought His Wellspring for My Thirst.

My Heart Reached Out to Know Him More
His Nail Scarred Hand Knocked on Its Door.
I Cried Out, "Jesus! Yes, Come In!
Lord, Take from Me All Stain of Sin."

He Came and Made My Heart His Home
I Gave Him Back His "Stolen" Throne
And Like the Wind You Cannot See
His Spirit Swept Inside of Me.

Where Death's Master Once Held the Key
A New Life Blooms Eternally.
Darkness Holds Its Threat No More!
For with His Blood ~ He Marked the Door

The Death Angel Knows Whose I Am.
"Pass Over This House!" Says The Lamb.
No Longer Fearing Final Breath
For Life, Himself, Has Banished Death.

Yes, Let His Blood Mark Your Heart's Door
And You'll Have Life Forevermore.

Monika Starr Langguth
In Honor of Passover
TGBTG ~ March 30th, 2000©

~ 27 ~
GOD'S THE BOSS

It's Time the Devil Learned Who's Boss!
Christ Took All Our Sins to The Cross!
He Took All Sickness and Disease!
In Jesus' Name Command They Leave!

The Devil's Words Are Filled with Lies
Against God's Children, He Still Tries
But We Can Walk in Health and Blessing
If Truth in God's Word We're Confessing.

Our God Is Lord of All That's Living!
So, Give Him Praise and All Thanksgiving!
He Is The One That Gives You Breath
He Gave His Life to Banish Death.

It Doesn't Matter How You're Feeling
By His Stripes You've Got Your Healing!
If Satan Tries to Sock It to Ya
You Just Shout Out, "Hallelujah!"

Yes! Stump "The Chump
Of the Dunghill Dump"
And an Exit-Left He'll Blaze.
Too Great A Sound
For That Hell Hound

Monika Starr Langguth

Are the High High Sounds of Praise!
No Longer Feeling' Down and Out
Our Healing's Here! Come On, Let's Shout:
"We've Been Redeemed from Every Curse!"
LET THAT ECHO THE UNIVERSE!!!!

Monika Starr Langguth
TGBTG
1990©

~ 28 ~
RAINBOW OF DREAMS

I Opened Up the Window
And Was Kissed with Lips of Spring.
Birds Coaxed Notes to Flood My Soul
My Heart Joined Them in Wing.

Bathed in Rain... The Childlike Blooms
Shared Shining Faces... Soft Perfumes
The Wind Called Them to Dance.
They Beckoned Me to Feel Their Joy:

"Don't Let Your Doubts Steal and Destroy"
They Whispered, "Take A Chance."

The Curtain Parted Long Enough
To Feel the Sun's Sensation
Raindrops Blend with Streams of Light
A Glorious Visitation.

And There in His Full Majesty
Prismatic Patriarch!
A Gift of Love from Up Above
Behold! A Rainbow's Arc.

Monika Starr Langguth

Red... For Passion and For Strength
Orange... Is the Flame
Yellow... For Life's Brilliant Light
Green... Means Life ~ Again

Blue... Is Heaven's Hopes and Dreams
Indigo... The Mystery
Violet... All That's Beyond Time
To Dare... Eternity!

The Vision's Gone... The Seed's Been Sown
To Send Forth Thought's Creation
This Is God's Child... Loved Best When Wild
Who's Named, IMAGINATION!

Monika Starr Langguth
TGBTG
1989©

~ 29 ~
TEMPUS FUGIT

Oh, Time, Oh, Time, Where Have You Gone?
In Restless Quest You Fly
It Seems the Sun Has Just Come Up
And Evening Draweth Nigh.

And As the Night Falls Deep And Full
Plans End I've Failed To See
At Last, I've Guessed Why God Thought Best
To Make Eternity.

Monika Starr Langguth
TGBTG
1988©

Monika Starr Langguth

~ 30 ~
SOUL/GOAL

You Take Care of Your Body
You Take Care of Your Mind
And What Will Live Forevermore
Seems Has Been Left Behind.

You Mock That Former Statement.
You're Proud! You've Met Your Goal
In Truth, You've Set No Goal at All
No Plan Made for Your Soul.

Your Body's Strong and Flexible
Its Full of Form and Grace
Youve Cared for That... And That Will Die
Your Soul? No Resting Place.

There's an Eternal Blueprint
It's Called The Master Plan
Available to All Who Seek
Boy, Girl, Woman and Man.

It Goes Beyond the Outer-Self
Or What's Called, Our Within
And Someday It Will All Be Judged
By Its Pureness Or Its Sin.

Gifts To The Giver ~The Early Years~

The One Who Made Your Body
You Mind, Your Heart, Your Soul
Is Jesus Christ...And Without Him
You Never Can Be Whole.

For You Have Rule Over These Parts
That Think and Breathe and Feel
But, If Your Soul's Not in Your Goal,
Youve Made A Fateful Deal.

Monika Starr Langguth
TGBTG
1996©

Monika Starr Langguth

~ 31 ~
LET THE HEART SPEAK

Love Is the Greatest Treasure
Your Heart Can Ever Hold
Though It Doesn't Cost A Cent,
It's More Precious Than Gold.

Love … Pure Love … It Is the Key
That Gives Your Heart A Voice
Yet, You Don't Have to Wait for Love
With Love, You Make A Choice.

So, If You Know That Loves the Thing
Your Heart Is Longing For
Choose to Give Your Love Away
And Love Will Fill You More.

Soon Your Heart Will Overflow
Perhaps This Is the Day
You Teach by Showing Someone Love
And Start Them on Their Way.

Fill a Heart That Once Was Hollow
And As You Fill, More Love Will Follow

Monika Starr Langguth
TGBTG
1996©

~ 32 ~
ABBA, WILL YOU HOLD ME?

Abba, Will You Hold Me?
Let Me Rest Within Your Arms
Then I Feel Your Love Enfold Me
I Am Safe from All Life's Harms.

My Soul Can See You Watching
Tears of Love Within Your Eyes
You Never Wants Us Wanting
All We Need Abba Supplies.

How I Love That I'm Your Child
And I Know You Love Me So
Hold Me Just a Little While
Abba, Never Let Me Go.

Then My Heart Hears as You Whisper
Something Loving in My Ear:
"I Am Closer than Your Heartbeat
You Will Always Find Me Here.

So Just Call Me and I'll Answer
Evermore I Am with You
There Is Nothing I Won't Give You
There Is Nothing I Won't Do.

Monika Starr Langguth

For I Want the Same Thing You Want
Love and Be Loved in Return
You Are My Own Precious Child
In My Heart, The Fires Burn."

Then I Sigh and Say, "I Love You"
From Your Lap, I Then Now Stand
When I'm Not Held in Your Great Arms
I Am Holding Abba's Hand.

For My Father Is My Father
That Is Who He'll Always Be
He Sent Jesus Christ My Brother
To Tell That Truth to Me.

And The Father Has a Message
From His Heart That's Ever True
He Sent Jesus Christ to Tell You
That You're Abba's Child, Too.

Monika Starr Langguth
TGBTG
2000 ©

Gifts To The Giver ~The Early Years~

~ 33 ~
~ BAA BAA ABBA ~

Baa Baa Abba
It's Your Little Sheep That Calls
Baa Baa Abba
You, The Lifter of Whom Falls.

I'm Lost - Caught in The Brambles
Shivering in The Cold
Then I Feel The Shepherd
As He Lifts Me Up to Hold.

He Softly Whispers in My Ear,
"Peace, Little One, For I Am Here."
He Comforts Me So I Don't Cry
And Sings Me Heaven's Lullaby.

He Tells Me I Must Be Aware
That There Is Still A Wolf Out There
But No Wolf Dares to Cross the Land
That's Guarded by This Shepherd's Hand.

This Shepherd Guards Us Like A Rock
His Watch Unceasing for His Flock.
So, If You Wander Off Too Far
No Matter Just How Lost You Are

Monika Starr Langguth

Just Call His Name and He'll Be There
To Lift You Up into His Care
You're Safe Within His Loving Arms
With Him There Are No Fears... No Harms

He'll Whisper, "Little Lamb, Don't Cry
You're Not Forsaken...
It Is I."

Monika Starr Langguth
TGBTG ~ 1995©

~ 34 ~
DO YOU KNOW THE TIME?

I Laid Down on My Bed One Night
And in The Dark... I Cried
Although, I Still Was Breathing
Deep Inside, I Felt I'd Died.

I Did Not Care If Nighttime Passed
Or Ever Came the Sun
I Felt That If I Breathed My Last,
It Mattered To No One.

Then Suddenly, I Wiped My Eyes
And Listened as In Shock
For in My Room So Deafening
I Heard A Ticking Clock.

I'd Never Heard That Sound Before
I Trembled Now in Fear
The Ticking Clock Intensified
It's All That I Could Hear.

Oh, God! I Cried, What's Happening?
My Hands Covered My Head
The Ticking Clock Grew Louder Still
It Seemed to Rock the Bed.

Monika Starr Langguth

Jesus, Help Me Now! I Screamed
The Ticking Clock? No More
I Jumped Out of My Bed and Dropped
To My Knees on The Floor.

The Silence Came Like Lightning
And Yet, I Felt Such Peace
A Voice Called from Within My Soul
As If in Sweet Release.

Fear Not, For I Am with You
You Are Never Left Alone
That Pounding Was Me on Your Heart
I Long to Make My Home.

I Feel Your Pain... Your Loneliness
I Know Just Why You've Cried
I AM The One Who Truly Cares
If This Night, You Had Died.

You've Heard of Me So Often
And Put Me Off So Much -
That This Was the Last Chance for Me
To Ever Get in Touch.

Gifts To The Giver ~ The Early Years ~

I AM The One Who Gives You Life
The One Who Sets You Free
Let Me Come and Live in You
And You'll Have Life in Me.

Jesus! Yes! Come to Me Now
And Live Within My Heart!
Let My Life Be Born-Again!
Please Give Me A New Start.

I Felt A Joy … A Love … A Peace
I'd Never Known Before.
I Just Regret I Took So Long
To Open My Heart's Door.

So, When You See or Hear A Clock,
Please Always Keep in Mind,
That If You Don't Know Jesus Christ
Then, Friend, This Is the Time!

Monika Starr Langguth
TGBTG - 1996©

Monika Starr Langguth

~ 35 ~
HELLUVA GAME

When You Play in Satan's Ballpark
With the Devil's Bat and Ball
You Haven't Got A Prayer, My Friend,
Not A Snowball's* Chance at All.

Sure Looks Like All is Going Great
At Least, That How It Seems
The Coach Tries to Convince You
That You're on The Best of Teams.

You're in The Starting Line-Up
Up to Bat and At the Plate
Perhaps, You'll Make "World Series"
Sad To Say, That Seems Your Fate.

"Swing That Bat," You Tell Yourself,
"Keep Your Eye on The Ball"
But When the Pitcher Throws It Out
You See No Ball at All.

"Strike One!" The Ump Yells Out Real Loud
And Then Calls Out, "Strike Two!"
You Say, He Never Threw the Ball!
Coach Says, "What Else is New!"

Gifts To The Giver ~The Early Years~

You Holler Out, "What's Going On?"
Ump Says, "Don't Yell at Me!"
And as You Turn Back to The Plate,
Ump Calls, "Yer Out! Strike Three!"

"Loser, In the Dugout!" Satan Screams
"You Stink! You're Busted!
The Best Mistake You Ever Made
Was That in Me You Trusted."

The Coach Just Stood There Laughing
With His Team Named, "Ship of Fools"
No One Wins at Satan Stadium
'Cause He Makes All the Rules.

*(old saying: "snowball's chance in hell)

Monika Starr Langguth
TGBTG
1990 ©

Monika Starr Langguth

~ 36 ~
THE TREASURE OF A FRIEND

There Are Many Treasures in My Heart
That Always Make Me Smile.
Some Are There A Long Long Time
Others Just A Little While.

The More Time My Heart Holds This Wealth
The More the Treasure's Worth.
Each Day, It Makes Me Richer Still
Like Nothing Else on Earth.

My Heart Has Many Treasures
And God's Helped Me to Find
That Each Treasure Is Quite Unique
And All One of a Kind.

Sometimes I Take These Treasures Out
When I Am Feeling Sadness
And Dwell Upon How Rich I Am
And Sorrow Turns to Gladness.
And Even If They've Left the Earth
My Heart Still Holds Their Precious Worth.

Monika Starr Langguth
TGBTG
1994©

Gifts To The Giver ~The Early Years ~

~ 37 ~
~TAME YOUR TONGUE ~

Your Tongue Should Stay Within Its Alley
Behind the Walls ... Before the Valley

If It Find Gossip Its Delight,
Those White Walls Should Take A Bite!

If It Blasphemes ... Or Makes A Liar
Take A Torch and Set on Fire!

If Only Wrong Things It's Confessing,
It's Lost Its Right to Use for Blessing.

It Can Cause Pain and Bring Destruction
Or Bring Great Joy with Gods Instruction.

If It Is Tamed ... Then Peace Will Follow
And If It's Not ... Its Best You Swallow!!

Monika Starr Langguth
TGBTG
1997 ©

Monika Starr Langguth

~ 38 ~
GRANDPA'S EYES

Even till Today
When I Look Back in My Mind
I Can't Remember When
My Grandpa Wasn't Blind.

I Always Was Quite Careful
Not to Leave Toys on The Floor
And Make Sure That I Put Things Back
Just Like They Were Before.

Grandpa Had A Little House
That He Kept Up with Pride
And Had A Dog Named, Oliver
That Stayed Close by His Side.

"Have You Seen My Roses?
Look! The Lilacs Are in Bloom!"
He Taught Me How He Knew They Were
By Their Beautiful Perfume.

And Sometimes on The Old Porch Swing
In the Darkness of The Night,
He'd Tell Me Though His Eyes Grew Dim,
His Heart Was Full of Light.

Gifts To The Giver ~ The Early Years ~

An Angel Goes Before Me
I'd Always Hear Him Say.
He Told Me He Saw Jesus
Every Time He Knelt to Pray.

I Loved My Grandpa Very Much
And I Was Just Eleven
When He Went Back Home to The Lord
And Joined Grandma in Heaven.

Mom and Daddy Got the House
And Everything Inside.
And Not Long After Grandpa Left,
Old Oliver Then Died.

Being the Only Grandchild,
His Bible to Me Came.
An Envelope Was Placed Inside
Addressed in Just My Name.

"Dear Child, I'm An Old Man Now
But, Thank God, I've Grown Wise
And Know the Best Gift I Can Give
Is Leave to You, My Eyes.

Monika Starr Langguth

Not the Ones That See the Trees
Or Clouds That Hide the Sun
But Eyes That See the Way of Truth:
The Truly Holy One.

For Though I Walked This Lowly Earth
And Had Become Quite Blind
I Saw All Through My Second Birth
With My Heart and Soul and Mind.

For Whether You Have Eyes or Not
You're Blind If You Can't See
Jesus Is The Only Light
That Shines for You and Me."

Many Years Have Now Gone Passed
With Joy My Heart Still Cries:
That My Grandpa Loved Me That Much
To Leave to Me, His Eyes.

Monika Starr Langguth
TGBTG ~ 1990©

Gifts To The Giver ~The Early Years~

~ 39 ~
~ THAT I MAY SEE ~

That Every Day I May See
More of The Person You Planned Me to Be

Like the Rose That Gives Life to Her Fragrance and Bloom
Or the Silvery Light from The Grandiose Moon

Or A Diamond That Sparkles When Held in The Sun
May My Life Be A Gem in Your Hand, Holy One.

Then I'll Hear at The Meeting of God and Of Man
Well Done! Enter In! You Have Followed the Plan!

Monika Starr Langguth
TGBTG
1996©

Monika Starr Langguth

~ 40 ~
~ I LOVE YOU … STILL ~

We Tied the Ribbons on the Trees.
There's Yellow Bows for Miles.
The Troops Would Know We Loved Them So
And That Would Bring Them Smiles.

We Took the Idea from A Song
That Was Written Long Ago
For Someone Who Had Been Away
And Just Wanted to Know:

That If He Was to Come Back Home
He Asked If He Might See
A Tree Where Yellow Ribbons Hung
"Oh, If You Still Love Me."

And Yes, To Show We Love Them So
That They Are Not Alone
We'll Tie A Million Trees or More
Until They Come Back Home.

Gifts To The Giver ~ The Early Years ~

Yet, As I Gave Thanks to The Lord
For All He's Brought Us Through
He Said, "Oh, There Is So Much More
I Long to Say to You."

And I Was Still and Let The Lord
Speak to Me Through The Spirit.
And This He Said, Those with Eyes... See
And Those with Ears... Now Hear It.

I Hung Upon A Tree for You.
I Died to Set You Free.
And There Is War Forevermore
Till All Come Back to Me.

Oh, Yes, Man's Fought A Fight with Man
But It Is Nothing More
Than A Teardrop in The Ocean
As to What Lies Soon Before.

The Cross Is Where the Battle's Held.
Where Satan Lost the Fight.
It's Where You Cross the Bloodstained Line
From Darkness into Light.

Monika Starr Langguth

I Am The Way... Just Come to Me
That Is My Heart... My Will
The Very Meaning of The Cross
Is "Yes, I Love You... Still."

As Long as There Are Souls Unsaved
In Our Hearts We Must See
A Yellow Ribbon Tied Around
The Tree at Calvary.

Monika Langguth
A Vision While My Son, A Marine, Was in Persian Gulf War
TGBTG
1991©

~ 41 ~
~THE PRODIGAL~

When Did You Fall from Grace, My Child?
When Did You Find It Was Time?
Thinking the Branch Could Live Unreconciled
That Severs Itself from The Vine?

The Branch for A Time May Seem Green and Strong
But, In Itself, Has Not A Root.
Though It Feigns Life . . . Its Last Breath Won't Be Long
For That Which Is Dead, Bears No Fruit.

A Branch Is Just That - It's A Part of The Whole
The "Whole" Is Christ Jesus . . . The Vine
Break the Branch from The Vine . . . Sunder Spirit from Soul
For Only in Christ Is Life Thine.

Beloved, If from The Vine . . . You May Now Be Broken
Seek God . . . And Repent . . . He'll Forgive
He'll Graft You Back to Him . . . For His Word Has Spoken
Forever . . . In Christ, You Will Live.

Monika Langguth
TGBTG ~ 1995©

Monika Starr Langguth

~ 42 ~
~ BECAUSE OF LOVE ~

It's Just Because I Love You
That I Feel We'll Part Someday
And I Will Go to Heaven
And You'll Go "Another Way"

Many Nights I Lay Awake
And Find It Hard to Sleep
Or Walk into Another Room
So, You Won't See Me Weep.

As Long as I Have Known You
I Have Loved You ... That Is True
And Never Want to Be the Cause
Of Bringing Pain to You

But I Feel You Get So Angry
When I Tell You of My King
That You Resent the Joy I Have
That Lifts My Heart to Sing.

Gifts To The Giver ~The Early Years~

It's Because The Father Loved Us
That He Sent His Son to Earth
To Ransom Back "His Stolen Ones"
(To God, We Have Great Worth.)

Because You Mean So Much to Me
And I Say This from My Heart
I Fear That in The Future
You and I Will Someday Part.

I Want to Share Eternal Life with You
And Leave You Never
For Jesus Promises, "In Him"
That We Can Live Forever!

It's A Sad Thing I Must Tell You
And to Say This Makes Me Cry
But, If Jesus Christ Is Not Your Lord,
Then Someday, We'll Say, "Goodbye."

Monika Langguth
TGBTG
1990 ©

Monika Starr Langguth

~ 43 ~
THE KING'S TEARS

I've Seen Great Sadness in This World
But I Think the Saddest Thing
Was The Vision Seen Within My Heart:
That of The Crying King.

"What Is It, Majesty?" I Asked
Then Heard The Spirit's Breath,
"I Want to Give Them Kingdom Life,
But They Choose Hell and Death.

They Fight to Grasp Illusive Dreams
For Earthly Things They Lust.
Instead of What I Long to Give.
They Choose Decay and Rust."

I Knelt... His Royal Warrior.
Although Upon This Earth,
A Soldier of The Highest Rank
Gained Through My Second Birth.

And in My Heart (His Palace Walls)
I Knelt Before His Throne
And God, My King, My Everything
Spoke... For I Am His Own.

Gifts To The Giver ~ The Early Years ~

"Go and Take the Cities
As You Never Have Before!
Go Forth! You'll Win the Battle -
For I Have Won the War!"

And There Within My Heart of Hearts
I Heard the Words He Thundered:
"Go to Those That Thirst for Truth
That Satan Long Has Plundered!

You Have All Power That You Need
To Let the Truth Be Heard."
He Pointed to My Two-Edged Sword,
"Your Weapon Is My Word!"

"Remember This," He Said to Me
"Whatever You Go Through,
There Is No Place... Or Man You Face
That I Am Not with You!"

I Will Go, Most Holy One
Your Will... I Choose to Do
This Life I Live... I Freely Give
In Service unto You.

Monika Starr Langguth
TGBTG ~ 1995©

Monika Starr Langguth

~ 44 ~
~ SISTERS ~

There Was A Garden in The World
That Grew the Sweetest Flowers
And People Came from Near and Far
To Gaze on Them for Hours.

The Tulips and The Daffodils
Were Picked and Cut for Window Sills.
And Some Were Placed in Bouquet Bunches
To Grace Tables at Ladies' Lunches.

But, In the Garden . . . Who Supposes
God Would Place Just Two Red Roses?
One Was Picked . . . But All Alone
A Crystal Vase Became Her Home.

How Beautiful the Flower Stood
As Made of Velvet . . . Yet of Wood.
And Day by Day . . . The More It Bloomed,
The Room Was Hauntingly Perfumed.

But, Oh, Too Soon, My Precious Rose
Began to Lose Her Regal Pose.
As Her Head Bowed . . .
You Must Now Pardon

Gifts To The Giver ~The Early Years~

Running Thoughts Back to That Garden
Where Once She Made Her Lovely Home
I Chose to Take Her All Alone
And Selfishly Seemed Not to Care

About the Rose Left Standing There.
I Wondered While My Rose Had Died,
The Bouquets Still Lived on With Pride.
I Think... I Know... I Must Confess

My Rose Died Out of Loneliness.
The Garden Rose? Yes, Mine Just Missed Her.
I Think That Flower Was... Her Sister.

So, Now When Flowers Come in Season
I Think God Plants Them for A Reason... Together.

Monika Starr Langguth
TGBTG
1990©

Monika Starr Langguth

~ 45 ~
~ OH SOLOMON ~

Oh, Solomon... If You Were Wise,
Why Did You Have So Many Wives?

And Though with Tongue Like Sharpened Sword
You Taught the Wisdom of The Lord
How Sad Within Your Fleshly Being
Had Not the Eyes for Truth in Seeing

Temptation on Your Heart Then Trod
And Loving 'Self,' Forgot Your God

Words Like Perfumed, Seasoned Herbs
"Gifts of God's Mind" In His Proverbs
Within an Impure Vessel Held
Unless... The Tree of Self Is Felled

We Start to Think That It's Our Fruit
Forgetting That God Is Our Root.
Wise Words to Keep Your Spirit Limber:
Swing That Ax and Shout Out, "Timber!"

Monika Starr Langguth
TGBTG ~ 1991©

I SEE GOD

Sometimes When the Day Is Done,
I Look at Stars and See "The Son"
And Feel the Joy the Morning Brings
When Through the Throats of Birds, God Sings.

And Then Again in Early Day
I See Him as The Children Play
Like Joyful Flowers Everywhere
I Feel His Peace… They're in His Care.

Still, When the Afternoon Has Come
He Warms Me in The Setting Sun
And So, His Love I Won't Forget
He Paints It in A Great Sunset.

He Lets Us Know from Up Above
He Promises His Watchful Love
Yes, All His Promises He Keeps
He Is The God That Never Sleeps.

He Lines Our Every Thought with Gold
If He, Within Our Hearts We Hold
For Nothing Life Has Can Compare
To Always Knowing He Is There.

Monika Starr Langguth

I See Him Everywhere It's True
Especially, When I See You!

Monika Starr Langguth
TGBTG
1990©

~ 47 ~
~ SALVATION ~

A Caterpillar Inched Along
Naive and Unaware
And Saw A Thing of Beauty
But in Truth, A Spider's Lair.

Dewdrops Glistened on The Lace
Like Diamonds in The Sun.
"Oh, How Beautiful It Looks!"
Thought Foolish Fuzzy One.

The Spider Hid Beneath A Leaf
So Not to Scare His Prey.
Then Quietly He Tip-Toed Off
To Trap Again That Day.

The Caterpillar, Mesmerized,
Crawled on The Silky Net
And Found The 'Diamonds' Ceased to Be
And Now His End … He'd Met!

Monika Starr Langguth

Something Deep Within Him Said,
"Quick Spin A Cocoon!"
And Faster Than He Ever Moved
He Built Himself A Room

The Little Fuzzy Fella Knew
That God Would Keep Him Well
Wrapping Himself Safe and Warm
Within This Silken Shell.

The Spider Sure of What He'd Caught
Came Back to Claim His Catch
And Found No Weapon That He Formed
Against This Shell Could Match.

Hiding in The Chrysalis
The Little Soul Grew Strong
Outside the Spider's Wondering
What on Earth Went Wrong?

Both Day and Night the Spider Waits
Then to His Sad Surprise:
God Frees the Captive from Death's Gate
And Out the Victor Flies!

Monika Starr Langguth
TGBTG,~ 1990 ©

Gifts To The Giver ~ The Early Years ~

~ 48 ~
STARGAZER ~

Oh, Stargazer, What Do You See?
When You Look at The Heavens, Do You See ME?

Are You Looking at The Oceans Turned Upside Down?
With Seashells Twinkling from A "Higher Ground?"

Are You Searching for Answers in Time and Space?
In Quest of a Fleeting Glimpse of MY Face?

Then Lenses of Glass from You Must Depart.
Use Your Inward Eye ... Search Within Your Heart.

For the Heavens Behold Just The "Gifts" Of ME.
For to Seek MY Face ... You Must Look in Thee.

The Sun Is A Star ... And A Dying One.
But The "Living Star" Is The "One True Son."

If You Seek MY Face ... There Is Just One Hope.
Use Your Inward Lens for Your Telescope.

Monika Starr Langguth

It's the Heart of Man Where I Long to Be
Look Within Your Heart ... If You Look for ME.

But, I'm Only There If I'm Welcomed In.
"Lord, Come Live in Me" ... That's Where You Begin.

Then Nevermore Will You Search in Vain
Deep Within Your Heart ... That's Where I'll Remain.

Monika Starr Langguth
TGBTG
2000 ©

Gifts To The Giver ~ The Early Years ~

~ 49 ~
~ STELLAR RENDEZVOUS ~

Star Without A Name.
Star Without A Face.
Whirling Through the Galaxies.
Spinning Off Through Space.

Searching Always for A Star
To Cast Its Light Upon.
Some Sparkled... Twinkled... Even Glowed.
Then Poof! Their Light Was Gone.

But God Had His Plan for This Star
To Fall Through Space A Time.
And If the Star Would Trust in Him,
The Gift Would Be "Divine."

If It Had Faith... And Traveled On
Forsook How Long or Far,
It Would Find Its Galaxy
Beside The "Waiting Star."

Yet, As It Spun in Endless Flight,
The Star Lost All Control.
Instead of Finding "The Pure Light,"
The Depths of The Black Hole.

Monika Starr Langguth

The Very Embers of Its Life
Were Sadly Growing Dim.
The Power to Continue On
Was Dying Deep Within.

"I Can't Go On!" Cried Out the Star.
But God Is Always True
And Placed Him With "The Star of Stars"
In Stellar Rendezvous.

It's When Life Seems the Darkest
And in Never-Ending Night,
Not Off Too Far... "The Waiting Star"
His Name Is "Life and Light."

Monika Starr Langguth
TGBTG
1990 ©

~ 50 ~
~ THE FALL ~

Saul Galloped to Damascus
With Hatred His Life Force
Until That "Great Light" Blinded Him
And Threw Him from His Horse.

A Sightless Self-Inflicted Doom
His Past No More Would Be.
"The Light" That Blinded "Saul" That Day
Would Now Cause "Paul" to See.

Sometimes In Love God Must Use Force
And Throw Our Pride Off Its High Horse.

Monika Starr Langguth
TGBTG
1988©

Monika Starr Langguth

~ 51 ~
FIRE-FIGHTERS

Long Time Ago, There Lived A King
He Wore A Crown and A Big Gold Ring
And Every Word That He Would Say
All the People Would Obey.

He Built A Statue of Pure Gold
(As Tall as Buildings Are, We're Told)
The King Then Passed the Word Around,
"Worship the Statue and Hit the Ground!"

Said Shadrach, Meshach And Abednego
"We'll Worship Only God!" And So,
The King Got Hot as Fire and Said,
"Into the Furnace till You Are Dead!"

Tied and Bound in The Big High Flames
Went Three Little Boys with The Funny Names
Seven Times the Flames Made Higher
The Servants Melted from The Fire.

The King Was Shocked at What He Saw
Within the Furnace... There Were Four?
He Rubbed His Eyes! "This Just Can't Be
I Know That There Were Only Three!"

Gifts To The Giver ~ The Early Years ~

Inside the Furnace, They Were Walking
And Looked as If They All Were Talking.
The True God You Can Always Trust
That He Will Always Be with Us.

King Nebuchadnezzar With the Big Long Name
Said, "Open the Furnace! Turn Off the Flame!"
He Was Frightened... It Was No Joke
The Boys Didn't Burn, Nor Smell of Smoke!

Said Shadrach, Meshach And Abednego
"We'll Tell You Again So You Will Know.
No Matter If It Gets Real Hard
We'll Only Worship The True God!"

The King Did Not Have to Think Twice.
"Boys, I'm Taking Your Advice.
And Make by Royal Declaration:
To Worship Your God Through This Nation!"

And So What Lesson Do We Learn?
Worship The True God...
You'll Never Burn!!

Monika Langguth
TGBTG
1990 ©

Monika Starr Langguth

~ 52 ~
BLESS OUR LITTLE HOME

Bless Our Little Home, Dear Lord,
Where All Our Hearts Can Come
And Rest in Peace and Sing Your Praise
When All Day's Work Is Done.

For in Our Little Home, Dear Lord,
Our Hearts Combine as One
And Thought the Veil of Nighttime Falls
We're Sheltered By "The Son."

So, Bless Our Little Home, Dear Lord,
And All We Say and Do
And May Our Hearts Long for Your Love
And Make A Home for You.

For When the One That Made Our Hearts
Can Dwell Within His Own
With Joy We'll Say … Both Night and Day
"That There's No Place Like Home."

Monika Starr Langguth
TGBTG
1990©

Gifts To The Giver ~The Early Years~

Monika Starr Langguth

www.ingramcontent.com/pod-product-compliance
Lightning Source LLC
Chambersburg PA
CBHW020143130526
44591CB00030B/180